Lamentations of a Child

LAMENTATIONS
of
a
CHILD

Joyce Wyche

iUniverse, Inc.
Bloomington

Lamentations of a Child

iUniverse books may be ordered through booksellers or by contacting:

iUniverse
1663 Liberty Drive
Bloomington, IN 47403
www.iuniverse.com
1-800-Authors (1-800-288-4677)

ISBN: 978-1-4620-6473-1 (sc)
ISBN: 978-1-4620-6475-5 (hc)
ISBN: 978-1-4620-6474-8 (e)

Printed in the United States of America

iUniverse rev. date: 12/06/2011

For my two daughters whose fervent love and support has been nothing short of inspirational. We have prayed together, fasted together, and restored each other in our faith walk. You are truly a blessing in my life. As you navigate through life I pray much success and happiness. I pray that you continue to grow strong in the LORD. You are my joy.

Preface

GOD's people experience so many different feelings. Sometimes we are up. Sometimes we are down. Sometimes we are strong. Sometimes we are weak. These emotions have been experienced by some of the prophets and disciples in the Bible.

Often we feel guilty for our many moods.

This can be so common with our growth. The important thing is to understand that this is part of our growth and we are not to linger too long in negative periods.

Even Jesus in the garden of Gethsemethe just before his crucifixion was sorrowful; however, he did not linger there. It is so very important not to linger in our pain, sorrow, disappointment, or any of the other negative thoughts that would keep us from going higher.

We each have great heights to achieve. Each step can produce some reluctance, but this reluctance is just a stepping-stone along the path of the many miles that lie ahead for us. The further we go the more the stones may become pebbles.

This is how we reach great heights of a strong, sturdy, faith walk.

Introduction

I have always had a deep love for GOD and His word. Although my mother and father did not attend church, my father taught us to pray every night before going to bed. We would kneel down and he would listen to us, correcting our mistakes. It was my aunt who took me to church with her on Sundays. I was in the choir and attended summer church camps. My appreciation for GOD and church flourished.

My maternal grandmother introduced me to the holiness church. The experience taught me to be accepting of all faiths. They were so different from the subdued practice of the Methodist church that I was accustomed to. It did not seem strange but it was different. I believe that these experiences prepared me for the fullness of the body of Christ.

The fullness of the body of Christ simply means that you are willing to put in effect the word of GOD. You are willing to witness and disciple.

My childhood was like most. I was always a deep thinker and that left me open to ponder life and what it meant. This naturally (for me anyway) took me to GOD and what he meant. When I was baptized, at age 13, I was sincere about what was taking place. I thought that this was the time for me to be a bit more serious about

GOD. I wanted my baptism to mean something and I expected to be different afterwards, but I was a little disappointed when that wasn't the case. Still my love for GOD was intact.

At the age of 15 I sat in study hall class and thought "God I want to marry you, I want to be your wife. I don't need a husband and I don't need to have children. I want to marry you". Then I thought, "I am not catholic, how can I marry GOD?" In that same period in time, that same class I later thought "maybe you want me to get married, maybe you want me to have children". I left that conversation with GOD feeling like I would still have a close relationship with him. It was around this age that I had read Roman 10:9, That if you confess the Lord Jesus and believe in your heart that you are saved, then you shall be saved. I believed that I had to utter it to be truly saved so I uttered the confession under my breath. From that point on I did not doubt my salvation. Some time later, still at 15 or 16, a minister asked me to deliver the message at a youth day program. How little did I know about the path that GOD was laying out before me? If only I had a mentor, someone to talk to about spiritual things.

In my early 20s I became very angry with GOD. I felt forsaken and forgotten. I felt as if GOD did not care about me. His words taught me that his thoughts are not our thoughts neither are our ways his ways, Isaiah 55:8-9. We never fully understand what GOD is working out in us and we never fully understand how the trials are refining and preparing us for greater things in Him.

In my late 20s I found my way back to GOD. I was on a mission. I was determined to let my light shine before men that they may see my good works and glorify my father, Matthew 5:16. I have not gotten angry with GOD since. Every trial that I endured I tried to see the big picture, but it was not always easy.

Over the years I progressed from sitting in the pews with pen and pad taking notes to delivering the message behind the pulpit. It has been a wonderful life. Several have accepted the call of preaching through our conversations. I don't brag or boast, after all, it is not about me. I simply say that I have been trying to sow seed in good ground and bring forth good fruit, Matthew 13:8. I have been trying to be a good witness and leave testimony of my witness. Still again I say, this walk is not easy but, I would not trade it for anything. I absolutely love it and everything about it. I don't know what I would do if I did not have this life.

I have much work to do and many lives to reach. I am always asking what should I do now GOD? Every job I take I ponder who am I supposed to reach here and/or what is my purpose here. Everything is about GOD's purpose. We are created to serve him, to please him, to worship him and to praise him. He doesn't need us for these things but it gives us meaning to life.

I believe Jesus when he said "The works that I do ye shall do also, and greater works than these shall you do", John 14:12. The distractions of daily living have kept us from these greater works. We are weighed down by jobs, church work, and family life to the point that we have little true time and focus for Jesus. We wake up and began our day in a rush and the pattern continues all day. We are exhausted when we finally get home from T-ball and piano lessons, seldom having quality time for GOD.

Every day is a brand new day. We get to start over. We get to benefit from the past but also begin anew. Jesus is our Rock. The foundation is laid firm, strong, unshakable and secure.

Amen, Amen, Amen

Table of Contents

LAMENTATIONS

A Rose, With All My Love

You sent me a rose GOD.
A beautiful single long stem rose.
It was in full bloom and
A beautiful shade of red.
It is such a blessing to know your love.
Just as the rose was in full bloom,
So is your love for me.

A Grain of Sand

GOD, I know that you are real.
I can't see you.
I can't touch you.
I can't taste you.
I can't smell you.
Sometimes I wonder if I hear you.
I know that you are real.
I know that you have me in the palm of your hand.
I am like a grain of sand in your hand.
You hold so many granules of sand,
Yet you know each one.
Each granule is individual and special.
You are real.
You are special.
You are a very real and special GOD.

Reconstruction

Thank you LORD for reconstructing my life.
I've been shattered like pieces of the finest China.
The pieces are large and small.
You, LORD, have taken me in your hands.
You are putting the pieces back together.
When you have finished with me it will seem so perfect.
Each piece will be in its place.
My life will be reconstructed.

Evidence, Come Forth

I want to come forth Father.
I need time alone.
I want to meditate and cry out to you.
You have blessed me with a great spirituality.
Now I want it to come forth.
I want the evidence to be seen.

The Purest Fear

The fear that I have for you GOD is a righteous fear.
Some say, "You shouldn't fear GOD".
This is where our wisdom and understanding begin.
Just as our Children should fear us, so should we fear you.
Just as our children know that if they do bad things they will
be punished, so must we know that you will chasten us for our
sin and inequities.
Just as children don't want to let their parents down, we too
must labor to avoid letting you down.
Just as parents have that "look" to set their children on course,
we too must realize that you are constantly "looking" at us.
Fear of GOD is not a bad thing.
It is heavenly and glorious.
Fear of GOD can help to keep us on track.
After all there are some of us who must fear our parents to stay
on the right course of life.
Where would we be without the Love and Fear of GOD?
Thank you GOD for giving me "the look".

The Sun And Rain

My most precious heavenly Father,

You shine your light so brilliantly.
How can I ask for more?
You rain your blessings down on me.
Like gusts of hail they pour.

But, yet I come boldly before your throne
Asking for more each day.
As I learn to walk to receive my crown,
Knowing the trials I must face.

Dear GOD, my LORD, on high,
Your tender love envelopes me,
Like rays from the sun so bright,
I feel warmly immersed so tenderly.

The trials of life are temptous,
They toss us to and fro,
Yet with each trial we are victorious,
And onward to battle we go.

Thank you GOD for the Sun and the Rain.

I Humble Myself

My life is full of challenges.
Forgive me GOD if I seem arrogant.
So many times I have to defend myself.
Not against enemies only but friends who want to be exalted and step on me.
Forgive me for not being humble,
Forgive me for feeling the need to justify who I am, or why I feel the way I do, or why I've done what I've done.
This has placed me in the seat of arrogance and I cheerfully and willingly removes myself from that seat.
I take the seat of humility, the seat of meekness.
LORD I take a seat prepared by Christ.

Set Me Free

The bitterness in my soul is pulling my spirit down.
It is manifested through anger, resentment and frustration.
My enemies attack me on all sides and my friends, yes my
friends as well as family.
They go on to tell me all that is wrong with me.
They are zealous to highlight my shortcomings.
They tear at my spirit and rip me apart.
Oh that I could release as my flesh desires, but I hold back.
I try to maintain temperance and yet get my point across;
All they will understand is flesh.
Oh how the bitterness rests in my soul.
If only they would leave me alone to deal with myself.
If they would look with spiritual eyes they would see how I
travail to get back to Christ,
Back to his fullness.
Oh if they could just look in a mirror.

Desperate Love

I wish I could hug you LORD.
I imagine myself sitting at your feet or laying my head on your lap.
I imagine myself so close to you, but unable to see your face.
Just being close to you is often enough, but there are times when my arms ache to embrace you.
The sensation in them is real.
I do realize that you see my desire and that you feel the longing in my soul.
I LOVE YOU GOD!

The Reality of a Smile

The pressure of a smile is great O LORD.
I was taught that as Christians we should always smile and not frown.
How much burden will men continue to put on us?
I know my life should not have sour days every day but everyday is not a smile.
How much guilt is heaped on us because we do not smile always?
I think of Elijah. Did he smile every day?
I think not, and yet he did not see death.
He was taken up and changed going toward the heavens.
What about Peter, John the Baptist and John whom Jesus loved?
Did they smile every day?
They walked with the savior.
What about Jesus?
There was no greater man on earth than he.
Did he smile every day?
I must release the pressure that says if we don't smile we are poor witnesses.
I must let go of the idea that Christians should always smile.
I must learn that we do have bad days and it's OK. I must learn from the bad days to live my life better, to counsel better.
I must remember that it rains on the just and unjust and to rejoice oft times, but we simply won't rejoice every day and especially not all day every day.
LORD this is a burden that is heavy to carry.

Gossip

Gossip is so destructive.
Pretend Christians seem to be the worst,
Eager to betray the confidences that are entrusted to them,
Swift to run and share them with others,
Preying on the lives of others,
They burn the phone lines up,
The zeal to want to tell eats them up inside,
What a strong demon gossip is,
It weakens and corrupts everywhere,
"Resist the devil and he will flee from you" says James 4:9,
To resist is to oppose,
It takes away the pleasure and gratification,
What pathetic people they can become when satan enters in,
Desperate to know what goes on in the lives of others,
Dying inside to spread the news that they have,
There is no shame in their heart,
There is no disgrace on their minds,
GOD how disappointed you must feel sometimes,
Pretend Christians with no remorse,
Their goal is to know and to tell the lives of others, Judging
others and looking less at self,
With so much sadness in the world,
It becomes joyous to live off the sadness of others.
What pathetic people some have become?
Who will put on the whole armor once again?
Who will be a true soldier?
Who will stand righteously with Christ?

Passion

GOD I just love you.

If I could soar on my love I would circle the world over
one million times and more.

My heart aches with passion for you.

I long to seek your face.

I long to serve you.

I long to be your vessel.

GOD, Oh how I really do love you.

GOD's Presence

GOD
Your goodness and mercy have always been with me.
You have kept me even through the trials.
Things could have been so much worse,
but you poured out mercy.
Thank you GOD.

You Are GOD

You are GOD.
You created the sun the moon and the stars.
You created me.
I didn't create you.
You are GOD.
I am a mere mortal.
Forgive me for lifting myself up.
I cannot compare you to me.
I cannot see into my future, but you know my destiny.
You are the almighty, ALL powerful, ALL knowing GOD.

Beware of Deception

Father, trials bring such pain and despair.
Hear me, O GOD, as I pour out my soul.
Sometimes as we go through trial and transitions of life we reach out for a loving hand.
We want so desperately to be understood.
We want to be accepted.
It's often during these times that we pick up those that are not good for us.
Those who don't have real love, compassion, nor understanding.
What we get are those who want to manipulate, abuse, control, slander, and pull down, just to name a few.
Jealousy runs deep and pierces the depths of their hearts.
Their love is so very icy cold and clammy.
They come with a warm smile and sometimes-soft words.
Their words may even sound like comfort, but behind it all is jealousy, resentment, hatred, envy, and covetness (just as an eye opener).
When we look deeper we find malice, deception, paranoia, insecurity, and so many other strong holds.
GOD what a disguise satan can wear.
I look deeply at self and say, "Well I haven't been all that I should have been."
Father through my trials why couldn't someone look beneath the hurt and understand why.
Why couldn't someone feel my pain with the hand of compassion?
Truly this trial helped me to be stronger.
LORD let me sow love, compassion and understanding.

Compassion, Understanding And Love

It pains me LORD to look back and see what I picked
up along the way.
Christians?
I think Not!
Self-serving spirits of unrighteousness have been
everywhere.
Father how satan has gained so much control in the lives
of your people, those who should be strong enough to
help others as they go through their trials.
LORD, all they can see is self.
Father how it hurts so.
Give me strength tolerance and endurance.
I have always given of myself to others but yet in my
time of need, few, if any, are faithful.
Still GOD, I will continue to be there for as many as
you send me.
Forgetting self and remembering Christ and how he
gave of himself.
Father only you can be there for some of your people.
Other people cannot help.
Perhaps I am one of those that only you can be there for.
Please massage my heart with compassion,
understanding and love.
Forever I will serve you and your people. Allowing
myself to be mistreated at times, but holding on to you
and looking high for my crown.

Transparency

O GOD, how I want to scream at the wicked and say, "I
see your evil ways."
My heart keeps me still.
My heart feels compassion, sympathy, pain and regret.
I am compassionate because I know there must be hurt,
pain and disappointment behind the wickedness.
I feel sympathy because often they can't see their evil
and when they do they don't have the strength or the
conscientiousness of mind to fight the evil.
I feel pain because I hurt for their torment and I regret
that I can't touch their eyes, heart or mind with my hand
and give them the revelation.
If only I could let them see as I see.
Oh Father, If I see this little in your people how much
more do you see,
In Us All?

My Spirit

How good it feels to have my thoughts back.
I realize that my thoughts are lining up with Christ.
How good it feels to think of responses that represent Jesus.
How good it feels to release much anger and bitterness.
I don't deny that there is more to accomplish but,
I do rejoice in that I feel the growth coming forth.
The turmoil that once tormented me subsides,
As soundness of mind presides.

Going Forward

Forgive me GOD for all my sins.
As I look back over my life I see corruption and I see how I
have corrupted the lives of others.
It's a frightening thing to come out of a deep sleep.
You see your past and all the things you've done.
You ask, "How can you forgive me"?
You ask, "How can you look at me"?
Dear GOD I even find difficulty in asking for forgiveness.
GOD please have mercy and forgive those who gave me bad
counsel.
Truly GOD they are your children longing for your love.
GOD, I try to make sense out of this period of my life and
cannot.
I can only go forward from here.
Leaving behind the fragments of my broken life,
I'm trying to rebuild.
I pray to be better and stronger.

Revived

O LORD
I feel as if I've awakened from a deep sleep.
I feel tired and exhausted as if the dreams have been deep and
relentless.
Father now as I awaken I am still dazed.
I feel myself drifting in and out of consciousness.
I long to become wide-awake.
I long to be fresh and alert.
I long for the nightmare to finally end.
My haze is swiftly ending and my return to life is real.
It feels good to arise and feel the dawning of a new day.
A part of my nightmare I have to forget.
I can remember only as a learning experience, but I must also
forget.
How I regret those that I have hurt as I look over that time.
How I wish I could go back and erase the pain.
I must go on.
I'm awake and it feels good.
I have to go forward and reach for all of today, forgetting
yesterday, and not anticipating tomorrow.
I have to enjoy every moment in time and today is that
moment.
Tomorrow is not promised and too far ahead.
Thank you for calling me from my sleep.
Thank you for experiences during my sleep.
Thank you for nightmares but GOD,
Thank you so much more for waking me up.
Thank you for your love.

Wisdom

Thank you LORD, for the wisdom that you have given me.
With much wisdom comes much grief.
To know and see so much is a load to carry.
This wisdom is an answer to my prayers,
But I realize that it brings much sorrow.
Knowing so much and able to share so little.
It leaves a heavy loneliness.
Man can't begin to understand the knowledge this wisdom unfolds.
To know things that are years beyond what can be imagined is such a lonely place to be.
In all this I thank you GOD for your wisdom.

To The Bone

LORD, I feel a smile in my heart.
I'm happy to find my spirituality.
I've longed to get back to this place.
Now GOD I aim to be stronger.
I feel the pleasantness in my bones.
All is well in me.
I find peace in my soul.

GOD, You Are Mercy

Oh GOD, how Great Thou art.
You could have taken me in my sin,
but you saw fit to let me live.
How selfish I have been.
I focused on me and my hurt and pain,
Paying little attention to the hurt and pain that I caused you.
You extended grace and mercy and yet I know that you didn't
have to.
Further than that is the realization that you really shouldn't
have,
But that is my judgment.
Oh, how far we are from understanding you,
so far from really knowing you.
We live our lives judgmental.
Judging others and ourselves.
Oh GOD, we are often so far from you.
GOD, "How Great Thou Art".

You Never Forgot Me

Father you never forgot me,
Even when I wasn't my best you kept your hand on me.
LORD how faithful you are and how faithless I have been.
Even in this you never forgot me.
The trials came from the left.
The trials came from the right.
I was so overtaken until I fell under the weight of it all.
But LORD, knowing that even then you kept your hands on
me gave me the determination to rise up.
I could shake off the load because it was not mine to carry.
Though I fell LORD,
Your love never did.
Father GOD you are so faithful and you never forgot me.

We

GOD as I lay on my bed of affliction
I didn't want to get up.
I wanted to hide.
I wanted to hide behind my wall of escape and stay for a
while.
I wanted to forget responsibility,
I wanted to forget cares,
I wanted to endure the pain and seek no cure.
"I", "I", "I",
What about those who love me?
What about those who need me?
What about those who depend on me?
What about those who look up to me?
This "I" can hurt so many.
NO more "I"!
Now it's "we" GOD,
YOU, Jesus, the Holy Spirit, and Me!
Now it's "We"!

Illumination

LORD, I feel the fire burning in the marrow of my bones.
My love for you is deep and wide.
My passion is like heat illuminating from my body.
Oh GOD if I could just pass on the passion that I feel.
If only I could spread it to your people.
Oh Father, what a blessed place of love this world would be.
Show me GOD where I should go.
Tell me LORD what I should do.
Teach me Father what I should say.

My Truest Love

The tears that I shed are tears of love.
My love for you my LORD, consumes me.
GOD I want so desperately to prove my love for you.
My attempts are wobbly at time but my intent is sincere.
O GOD, Father, my LORD, I want to have a love affair
with you.
GOD how corrupt that must seem, but I love you so very
much.
This is a love that no man can touch.
I have carried this love since my youth, beginning at age
thirteen blooming at age sixteen.
Dear GOD you are my truest love.

Sincerity

Please help me find my way O GOD.
Lead me to do thy will.
Help me to fulfill your purpose for me.

Peace

GOD,

I thank thee Father for all that thou hast given me.

I stake full claim on it.

You have given me such peace.

This peace is mine.

I am grateful to you for it.

I belong to you, so does this peace.

Just as I am yours, one whom satan can't have, so is this peace.

Those things that belong to you he cannot claim.

He cannot claim me nor can he claim anything that you have given me.

I stand firmly rooted and grounded on that revelation.

Thank You GOD for Peace.

Undying Love

GOD,
My desires for you are strong.
I wish that I could put into words exactly what I feel in my heart.
My flesh yearns to be close to you.
I want to be an example of your goodness.
I want to live in uprightness.
I want to reach to the heavens and communicate with you.
GOD my love for you will never fail.
Though I will be persecuted or abused,
my love will stand.

Propel Me

Please forgive the evil that I possess in my heart, Father.
I am but flesh and corrupt.
I have great weaknesses.
I feel inept, incompetent, and inferior.
Have mercy upon my soul.
I desire to do better, to be better.
I desire to possess sincerity of heart.
Purge me LORD.
Give me strength to move forward.
Give me determination to go higher.
Give me perseverance to hold on until the end.

All I Know is You

GOD,
Thank you,
I pray that I can feel you today.
I pray that I will walk upright.
Sometimes I feel sorry for myself.
Sometimes I feel forsaken.
Sometimes I feel cursed.
Sometimes I feel downhearted.
I can't stop living for you.
It is so engraved in me.
Even if I had to crawl I would continue on for you.
It is so deeply embedded in me.
It's all I know.

Who is My Companion?

Father the passion that I feel
I want to share with someone.
Who is my mate?
Who is my companion?
Who is my spouse?
Who can be on one accord with me?
Who can understand my love and desires for you?
Grant, O GOD, that I may soon be joined as one with my
companion, my mate, my spouse.
Let our love embrace you, and let our love be embraced by
yours.
Let our love be an everlasting flame to ignite others with
love for you.
AMEN AMEN

I Want You GOD

Father, what is it that your people want?
Do they want church, service, Christ, or you?
Do they want all of those things?
Service is something anyone can do in any capacity.
Church is a place where anyone and everyone can go with
no commitment.
Christ is willing to be an intercessor for all.
You want all of your people to come to you.
What do your people want?
Do they want it all or just part?
With service come little.
With church come little.
With Christ come all.
With YOU come all.
What do your people want?

Seek And Find

Father what am I?
Who Am I GOD?
My soul is searching for an answer and I find none.
What is my direction?
Purge me from unrighteousness O LORD.
Perhaps then I can find answers.
I seek my identity.
I seek my direction.

Determination

I look over my life GOD with hearty disdain.
The shame and humiliation that I feel cannot be measured.
My path forward seems dim, but
I continue fighting to find my way.
Nothing can hinder me from reaching my goal.
Nothing can stop me from seeking your face.
Nothing can stop me.
Nothing.

Deception is Interference

GOD,

When I try to make a decision about my life someone comes along and tries to change it.

Satan has been so effective in keeping me unstable and off balance.

Not any more LORD.

He has kept me from trusting and believing in myself, but he will not hold me down any more.

Now GOD it's you and me.

Together we will defeat satan.

Stability and a balanced life are mine.

I Want to be Worthy

Speak to me GOD.
Please help me to see my worthiness.
I have prayed so much in times past, but I was out of your will in my living.
I know my prayers were ineffectual.
Now as I get my life in order I fear that my prayers are still ineffectual.
I am afraid to ask for anything for fear that I am not yet in good standing with you, and you will not hear me.
I want desperately to pray and ask for a breakthrough but I'm afraid that this prayer will be unanswered.
I want to be in good standing with you.
I want to pray effectual prayers.
I want to be righteous.
Please help me to see my worthiness.

One With You Father

Dear GOD,
You are so much a part of my life.
I can feel you so strong inside me.
I want to let you illuminate from inside me to outside.
Dear GOD you are so strong in me.

Loneliness

With all of the anointing that I have in my life,
with all of the anointing,
Why can't I see my life clearly?
I seek but have trouble finding.
I desire to know but it seems to be hidden.
Why can't I see my companion?
Why can't I see happiness there?
Am I to be alone?
Am I to not have a helpmate,
or be a helpmate to one?
Why must I feel such pain from loneliness?
Who is there for me?
Who have you appointed as my mate?

A Promising Future

LORD, I hear your voice say,
"You must be patient".
I hear you tell me my way is being paved, Things are being worked out.
I see in a vision that things will get better and my life will be prosperous.
I see your hand in my life as I haven't seen in seasons past.
You have always been with me,
But now things are different.
Your presence is different.
I know that you will lead me in a plain path.
Father I see more peace ahead for me.

I'll Follow You GOD

GOD I desire to close my eyes and take your hand.
I desire LORD to go wherever you lead me.
I don't want to stick my hand out and feel my way as you lead me.
I don't want to feel with my feet.
I want to walk in confidence knowing that you will lead me in a clear plain path.
You won't lead me to stumbling blocks.
I can trust you.
If I just let go of myself and trust in you, my walk would be smoother.
Not without trials as I make my stops, but I trust you to work it all out.

Take Me Up

Take me up dear LORD in your loving arms.
Take me up to fly around your throne.
Take me up dear LORD to that heavenly place. Take me
up where there is no wrong.
Death is not what I want right now.
I want to remain on this earth,
But let my spirit just soar on high,
Because I rejoice in my new birth.
Take my spirit and let it fly.
Let it praise you and worship your name.
Let me feel the beauty of your splendors in heaven.
Pleasing you GOD is my aim.
I want you to be so proud of me
As I walk down your narrow path.
Just take my spirit for just a while.
I know that your word says just ask.
Take me up dear LORD to be with you.
Take me up and let me soar.
Take me up dear LORD for a moment in time.
Take me up in the spirit once more.

Jesus Says

Jesus says, "I love you Child".

Jesus says, "In me there is no guile".

Jesus says, "Take my hand".

Jesus says, "Come to the Promise Land".

Jesus says, "There's joy and salvation".

Jesus says, "Let me give you the revelation".

Jesus says, "There's rest with me".

Jesus says, "I'll set you free".

Jesus says, "In me there is power".

Jesus says, "You'll bloom like a beautiful flower".

Jesus says, "I am the way".

Jesus says, "Come to me today".

Jesus says, "I am the life".

Jesus says, "I am the Christ".

Jesus says, "HE gave me the key".

Jesus says, "You can come only through me".

Jesus says, "I'm calling you today".

Jesus says, "Don't loose your way".

Jesus says, "I'll be your friend".

Jesus says, "I'll be with you to the end".

Remember Me

Dear GOD,
Be with me this day,
As I fall on my knees and pray.
I need you to take away the pain,
So that I don't go through again and again.
I want you to be the strength of my life,
Simply because I know I'm your wife.
Dear GOD my love for you is real,
Only you can know what I feel.
My heart's desire is revealed to you,
Help me to make my every dream come true.
The very thing that I yearn inside,
Is to be like Jesus who was a true guide.
I want to be like the prophets Elijah and Elisha,
And I can't forget Samuel, Ezekiel, and Jeremiah.
I want to walk in the faith that they had,
I want to posses all the good and not the bad.
And GOD as you draw me into this,
Remember I'm flesh and ease the pain with a kiss.
Please ease the pain because it hurts so,
Dear GOD ease the pain as I try to let go.
I want to make you so pleased with me.
I want to be all you want me to be.
Dear GOD remember me this day,
Remember me as I journey on my way.
Remember the love that I posses.
Remember my desires that I confess.
Remember dear GOD to soothe the pain,
Remember to be gentle again and again.
I love you dear GOD and I know that you love me.
Please be kind as my spirit becomes free.

Zeal

Excitement and joy flood my soul.
Time seems to be standing still.
GOD I want to run for you.
I'm in a hurry.
I want to learn more of you and nestle in my ministry.
Time seems to be standing still.
The months ahead will seem like years.
How I long to go forth but,
but how patiently I must wait.

A Fool for Christ

GOD,
I want so much to achieve a strong spirituality.
I want to wake up and have a new strong spiritual life.
I want flesh to die.
I want the devil to depart.
I want spirituality.
There is no one I can talk to,
No one who really understands.
What I want is not easy.
It brings much pain,
But it's worth it.
Is this a realistic dream GOD,
Or is it idealistic?

The Survivor in Me

GOD, you made me a survivor.
Not for myself,
But for others.
Although my enemies try to pull me down,
They attack on all sides.
The darts come fast through the air,
I catch them in my hand.
My adversary labors to torment me.
If I am pulled down it is for
but a while.
GOD, you made me a survivor,
Not for myself alone,
But for others.
Not only will I survive, but I will thrive until my work is
done.

The Intercession in Me

Dear GOD,
I want to intercede for your people.
There is much pain.
There is much hurt.
There is much disappointment.
There is much frustration.
GOD, I want to intercede on behalf of your people.
I want to bring them peace, love joy, and happiness.
Trials will come and
trials will go,
but Father let the love, joy, peace, and happiness
<u>Continually</u> envelope your people.

My Enemies, My Friends

Father,
Please forgive my enemies for all they have done to me.
Father please lay their transgression not to their charge.
It is not my desire that they go through the things that I have gone through.
Father they have come unto you.
They have taken up their cross, so please GOD make their path clear in this wise.
Your word teaches that a man will sow what he reaps, but GOD they have come unto you to serve you.
This world is filled with pain.
Filled with reaping, but GOD please don't let my enemies that are seeking your face reap what they have sown unto me,
Because you see GOD
They are no longer my enemies,
They are my friends.

GOD, You're Wonderful

What a wonderful GOD we serve.
You take away our anger.
You take away our hatred.
You touch our hearts with your healing hands.
You place in us love.
You place in us forgiveness.
You place in us peace.
What a wonderful, wonderful, GOD we serve.
You give us revelations.
You give us inspiration.
Only you GOD can make our enemies our friends.
Only you GOD can cause a bad situation to be good.
What a wonderful GOD we serve.

It's Time

It's time to be about my Father's business.
It's time to put all toys aside.
It's time to be a witness.
It's time to hold up the banner and not hide.

I Owe You Father

GOD you've been so good to me.
You extended your grace and mercy.
You saved me.
You even allowed me to enter into your ministry.
My life has been less than pure, clean or holy,
But not only did you <u>not</u> turn me away,
But you placed me in your ministry.
Now I owe you my life.
Every day is yours.
I want to live holy.
I want to be righteous.
I want to be of service to you and your people.
I want to heal your people GOD.
Father, I owe you all of me.

Look At Self

Living for you LORD is not easy.
There are many things I must give up and many sacrifices I
must be willing to make.
The love of GOD is great and unbinding.
Your love is proven daily.
You show me great and precious love.
What about me?
What about my love for you GOD,
And your sweet son, my precious savior, Jesus Christ of
Nazareth?
I must re-access and re-evaluate my love for both of you.
Let me look deep, deep, deep, within myself.
Not deep in others,
But deep within myself.

Spiritual Travelers

We are spirits in a body.
Heaven is our home.
We are on this earth for a short time,
Just as Christ was here for only a while.
We are to serve GOD,
To please GOD,
And to edify Christ.
Heaven is our home.
A spirit is light and has no weight.
We too must be light and carry no weight.
The weight that our bodies feel we must release.
We must not give in to the pain our bodies feel.
Truly we then allow the spirits of illness and disease to stake
a claim on our home.
We must not give in to the temptations that our bodies
instruct us to.
We must remain spiritual,
So spiritual until we separate ourselves from this world.
We are in this world but not from it.
We are truly pilgrims.
We are truly travelers in a strange land.
We are truly children of GOD.

Pulling At Your Garment

When we step into the fullness of the body of Christ,
When we begin our Christian walk,
We have many people pulling at our garment.
Although we can't see this with our natural eye,
virtue is taken from us.
As this happens in our lives we must reach back for strength.
Although we must fill that empty place from whence the
virtue is gone.
How do we fill it?
With an increase in our study of the Word,
With an increase in our prayer life,
With more frequency in fasting,
And/or with deeper conversation with GOD.
There are many ways to replace our virtue.
We must have determination to refill it.
We must keep striving, because the stronger we get in GOD,
The more people will pull at our garments.
Rejoice!!

Lift Me

The trials of my life have been so overwhelming.
I feel as though I've fallen,
And that my faith has failed me.
I know that I still believe and trust in your word,
But for a few precious moments I lay down my Sword.
Renew my faith.
Mend my wounded soul.
Lift me from this weight that keeps me from being whole.

Search Me

Search me LORD.
You've tried my soul and through your love and grace I've
been victorious,
I held on to my relationship with you.
Now LORD search my heart,
And see my every desire.
For in my heart you will find a great zeal to do great things for
you.
LORD, I'm patient enough to wait on your word to tell me
when to go.
Just search my heart LORD
And know that I wait.
I desire greater spiritual knowledge, strength, wisdom,
courage, faith, understanding,
And prosperity in all these.
Search me LORD.
You know my heart,
keep me pointed in the right direction.
Headed down that straight and narrow path.
Search me LORD.
My desire is to bud forward as a rose that will never die.
Allow me to serve you in great heights,
And perform your wondrous works.
Only then can I exemplify my deep rooted love and adoration
for you in a brand new way.
Search me LORD.

GOD is Faithful

The GOD that we serve is ever so wonderful.
When we are down,
And certainly we must all feel down sometimes,
He comes at just the right time to lift us up.
When we feel forsaken,
As all GOD fearing people do,
He will reach in with his gentle hands and touch our hearts.
When we feel the need to escape and run with tears in our
eyes,
He will stretch out his hand and embrace us with his love.
He is not a GOD to make us feel hopeless when we are
down.
He is not a GOD to make us feel deserted when we feel
forsaken;
And He is not a GOD to make us feel silly or guilty when
we want to run.
He is always there to give us hope,
Make us feel loved,
And take away our feeling of loneliness.
Our GOD is a GOD of compassion, Understanding,
patience, and most of all Love.
Thank you GOD for your Love.
Thank you GOD for your Love.
Thank you GOD for your Love.

Running the Race

I feel you pulling me GOD.
You are taking me so fast.
There is lost time to make up
And you are swiftly pulling me.
I know there is much to do.
I've put my life on hold
And now you want me to work.
GOD I'll willingly put my shoes on.
I'll go for you Father.
I'll absorb everything and retain what I learn.
I'm more than willing GOD.
I'm zealous.
Please GOD, make my path straight.
Please work out all the details.
All of the potential problems,
All of the hindrances,
All of the distractions.
I'm willing to go GOD.
I have put my shoes on.
I'm ready to run this race to the end.

The Potter's Plant

GOD you have rooted me up from my old place.
You have planted me once again in a place where my
growth can continue.
Like a plant I too was in a pot.
Just as plants outgrow it's present container,
I need a larger pot with space to grow.
Sometimes you will re-pot us in a different place for our
growth.
There are some who suit their pot,
There are others who must be re-potted again and again.
Father criticism runs high, but
LORD let your work in me be done.
I desire tremendous growth and
If I must go through many containers to get there,
Please let me grow.
To stay in a vessel too small,
Will mean either a stunted growth,
Where I will not achieve my greatest beauty, or
I will die for lack of space adequate enough to meet my
suffering needs.
Please GOD, re-pot me as often as it takes,
In whatever it takes.
Please GOD, allow me to grow and
Reach my beauty in you and Christ.

Changes From Growth

Father you have moved some distractions from my life.
All of those things that have hinder your divine purpose
for my life.
You have moved people, things, and situations.
Although these moves may be temporary,
They are truly necessary.

Stones for the Building

Jesus I'm working on my building.
You are the chief cornerstone.
The disciples are stones for my building.
The saints are as well.
The apostles are also there,
Gently laid to add their strength.
Jesus this building of mine
Is made from the very best.
I too, am a stone for this building.
There is a place just for me
When the time is right.
I too, will be laid in my proper place,
Adding to a solid foundation.
With you as a cornerstone, and
Others gently laid.
I am proud to be a part of this building of which
You, Jesus, are the chief cornerstone.

A Fresh Day

Thank you GOD for a fresh day.
Every day is a new day,
But not every day is a fresh day.
I feel renewed, revived, alert and eager.
Some days are difficult to get out of bed.
On those days I feel lack of motivation,
Low energy,
And just plain useless.
On a fresh day my body feels energized.
My head feels clear,
And I roll out of bed with excitement.
Thank you GOD for A Fresh Day.
It's new and exciting.
A Fresh Day!

Foolish Talk

GOD sometimes I dread being confronted with vain babbling.
The empty words.
The conversation fillers.
Sometimes LORD I am weary of the conversation of man.

Abuse For The Crown Of life

Dear Father
I suffer at the hands and tongues of many.
I want to maintain peace.
I want to hold on to the gift of temperance.
I used to feel anger but
Temperance has taken control.
Now I feel frustration.
How weak I must seem to all.
How powerless.
How vulnerable.
Still your temperance illuminates.
Man will never know how sometimes
I want to lash out
Just to show my strength.
This strength is the strength of flesh.
I must continue in the spirit.
Dear GOD, how foolish I must seem.
For you LORD I will be foolish.

Burdens Lifted

LORD I'm happier than I've been in a long time.
I thank you for that happiness LORD.
I feel as if I have been revived.
I feel as though a ton of weights have been lifted from me.
I can certainly go on.
I can certainly go forward.
Thank you LORD for lifting me.

Tongues

The words of a foolish Christian
Can be brutal in content and context.
Often things are said through ignorance.
It can show insensitivity
As well as lack of knowledge.
A loose tongue befalls us all at some point,
But a foolish tongue
Often befall some most of the time.
Oh how Christians must pray.
Christians should ask GOD to tame their tongue.
According to James 3:8, the tongue can no man tame.
This request must be put before GOD.
How ineffective our witness becomes.
Christians should travail in prayer for their own tongues.
Foolish Christians with foolish tongues.

Intimacy

What I want GOD!
What I really want,
Is to bask in your beauty,
Bask in your splendor!
I want to feel your arms envelope me!
I want to have the most
Intimate of intimate relationships with you!

Up and Out

GOD forgive me for seeming hard hearted,
But put my enemies to shame.
Those that rejoice over my trials,
LORD let their rejoicing be their pain.
Lift me up Father from the pit I am in.
Point me in a clear direction.
Let joy fill my soul.

I Give it to You GOD

Father all of my concerns are
In your capable hands.
Although my adversary would desire that I worry,
I release it all to you.
You, GOD, are everything to me.
You are my Father.
My battle is yours.
I know that you will fight for me.
All of my cares, my concerns, and my doubts,
I give to you.

Who Am I

Who am I GOD
that you are even think of me?
Am I worthy?
LORD I will labor
to prove my worthiness.
Happy am I,
to be a child of GOD.

Victory

I walk in defeat,
I profess defeat,
My faith is weak,
My fight is faint,
Now I rise up.
I stand firm.
I believe,
I trust,
I fight.
I am not helpless anymore.
I stand firm in faith.
I believe in my faith.
I trust with faith.
I fight with faith.
I am not helpless anymore.

A Faithful Servant

I do love your people LORD.
I don't want to inflict pain upon them.
I want to be encouragement and strength to them.
Father I don't want to let them down.
Your people are precious GOD.
I don't want them to be dismayed.
They look to me GOD.
I want so desperately to be there for them.
I don't want to turn away.
I see the desperate need in their eyes.
They reach out and hold on to me.
Oh GOD, I don't want to fail you.
I don't want to let you down.
Equip me Father with what I need,
So that I can effectively be there for your people.
It brings tears to my eyes.
I don't want to hurt them.
I want to help them stand.
Help me, Oh LORD, to be a vessel.

Overwhelming Goodness

Sometimes what I feel
In my soul I can't explain.
It just overwhelms me.
It's a feeling of goodness and blessing.
Sometimes I just want to cry.
I want to cry tears of joy, thanking you for your goodness.
It is such a good feeling.
Everything is going to be all right.

Perfection

I want to live my life holy.
I just want to live my life upright.
I don't want to get caught up in sin.
I don't want to give in to temptation.
GOD I just want to walk a perfect walk.
I want to go away to a quiet still place.
A place where I can lose myself in you.
I would meditate day and night.
If I could steal away time and time again.
Just being with you in peace would be my joy.
Oh GOD, how I long for perfection.

Father, I am Yours

My life is so completely yours GOD.
Everything that makes me who I am.
My spirit
My heart
My mind
My body
My soul
Everything about me.
Every vein
Every artery
Every muscle
Every tissue
Every bone
Every cartilage
GOD all of me I give to you.

Spiritual Growth

As we grow spiritually Father,
Help us to realize that we all start as embryos.
We come to our spirituality and must be born.
It should be considered a wonderful event.
Being born again is the beginning of our lives.

LORD we realize that because our spirits are so tender we
must receive formula first.
Newborn babes must desire the sincere milk of the Word (II
Peter 2:2).
As we grow in our infancy we also digest pabulum and other
baby foods.
We can't digest the hard stuff yet.

Growing in life takes us to table food.
Some can take table food sooner than others.
We also get to enjoy hamburger.
The best meat, steak, is soon to come.

We go on through life into puberty and adolescence, those
trying teenage years.
This is a crucial point of our life.
The pressure can overwhelm us.
We must learn to stand on our teachings.
We desire independence, but lack experience.
We are more vulnerable to the things of this world.

From these trying times we become young adults.
Spiritually we begin to leave the nest.
We enter into greater teaching, greater learning, and an opportunity to move out a little more.

Finally we have arrived!
It's time to enter into our ministry.
It's time to minister to more lost souls.
We have spent much time in preparation.
It's time to venture out into the call that we so obediently answered.

Not all will leave home.
Fear and insecurity will grip some.
A smart child will always know that he or she is never too old to learn.
Our spiritual growth continues yet still.

Forever And Always

I love you GOD.
Please visit with me in the wee hours of the night.
Keep my love for you fresh.
Keep my love for you alive.
Let me feel your presence in my life.
Forever and always.

GOD's Vessel

I want to speak your uncompromising Word GOD.
I want to build up where you instruct me,
Tear down as you direct.
I want to give love as you inspire.
I want to offer compassion as you lead.
GOD I want to be the servant among servants,
Lending myself to you as I walk this earth.
I am a vessel to be used by you, GOD.

Anointed

I feel your anointing GOD.
It is such a special touch.
At first I didn't know what it was,
But now I am sure.
Father what a blessing this is.
You want so much of me,
And all of me I give.
You are calling me closer.
I want to meditate on your voice.
I want to walk in the calling wherein I am called.

The Spiritual Walk

The Master's working hands have redeemed me.
I've been saved by the Master's working plans.
I've been washed in the blood of the crucified lamb.
Now that I'm in Christ I am a new creature,
Old things are passed away, and all things are new.
Now I follow his plan and take his hand.
I walk in the Spirit as he has instructed me.
Thank you LORD for being my creator.

Tears

Dear GOD, I've cried a bucket of tears.
　　　I've cried so much I'm drained.
　　　I've cried and cried for many years,
　　　I've cried to ease the pain.

Dear GOD Why have I cried and cried so much?
　　　Why have I been tormented?
　　　Why haven't I felt your tender touch?
　　　Why GOD? I know I've repented.

Dear GOD Is it because I never let it go?
　　　Is it because I kept holding on?
　　　Is it because I kept telling you no?
　　　Is it because I said your way was wrong?

Dear GOD I know now I never trusted you.
　　　I know my faith was weak.
　　　I know now what I must do.
　　　I know my faith must peak.

Dear GOD I know that I don't have to cry.
　　　I know that I can rejoice.
　　　I know that I can hold my head up high.
　　　I know trusting you is my choice.

GOD, My Love

Dear GOD,
I feel so much love
for you deep inside.
Within my heart
there is no place for pride.
Your gentle arms
I will never touch,
but within my heart
I imagine so much.
A tender kiss
I will never feel,
but oh dear GOD
I know that you are real.
Most of all
I want you to know
that my love for you
will continue to grow.
Dear GOD, My love,
As I end this prayer,
In the name of Jesus
Please don't end our affair.

Born Again

It feels so good to be born again.
My spirit indeed feels free.
No more am I a slave to sin,
I discovered that Jesus is the key.
Now when I fall on my knees and pray,
I feel it deep in my soul.
In GOD's protection I will always stay,
longing to remain in his fold.
Being born again makes me feel so light.
My Spirit just wants to soar.
No burden to weigh me down at night.
I look forward to what GOD has in store.
But most of all being born again,
I know GOD loves me so,
I accepted Jesus as my personal friend.
These are relationships I'll never let go.

Strive Don't Struggle

When you feel burdened down, as if trials come from near and far.
When you feel heavy-laden,
as if every day is a constant war.
You must stop and stand in battle;
You must look to the Word and make your plans.
You must cry out for help in Jesus and stop trying to be a god and just stand.
When you go through a fiery trial, say "LORD I acknowledge your work".
Every trial brings about new strength and there's something in you that GOD is about to birth.
So don't faint, struggle, and get weary.
Instead sing, dance, and shout praise.
Thank GOD for what he is doing in you,
because he is preparing you for another phase.

PRAYER OF OBEDIENCE

Dear GOD:
I want so very much to obey
Your tender voice no matter what you say
I want to be obedient to you
And do all the things you want me to do
I want to shed doubt and fears
I want to rejoice in my obedience with tears
Tears of joy because I've obeyed your voice
Tears of peace because I'll feel no remorse
I want to go where you tell me to go
My obedience to you is not to exalt just for show
To obey you dear GOD is a blessing for me
Because then I become all you want us to be
Obedience is better than sacrifice
Your word teaches me that with sound advice
I ask you this in Jesus name
Because through obedience I will feel no shame
Dear GOD as I close this prayer today
Place in me a spirit determined to obey.

I WANT

Dear GOD:
I come to you in prayer
Because all my burdens you can bear.
I want so very much to grow
Because with all my heart I love you so.
I want to feel your tender touch
And give you the praise you deserve so much.
I want to do your perfect will
And for you go over mountains, valleys and hills.
I want to stand and preach salvation
And help your children resist temptation.
I want to teach your holy way
To prepare so many for that great day.
Oh GOD, I want to walk your walk
And please dear LORD let me talk your talk.
Most of all I ask of you,
Let me do what you want to do.
In Jesus name I ask you this
Knowing LORD that with Jesus I just can't miss.
Remember GOD I love you so
And your gentle hand I'll never let go.
AMEN

Soaring

There are those Father whose desire is to keep me on their level.
They want to hold me down,
But you GOD have shown me that I can soar.
No man can hold me down LORD.
What you have done in my life is a blessing and I go wherever you lead.
Father I know that you will take me higher and higher.

My Porcelain Treasure

Father, help me to be careful with my mate.
Life can cause us to become busy.
Sometimes we take our treasures for granted.
My mate is like a valuable beautiful porcelain piece.
I don't want to put it on a shelf to collect dust.
I don't want to ignore it or place it far in back of other
things.
I don't want to handle it carelessly and drop it.
If it falls due to carelessness it may shatter.
I will do my best to glue it back.
The cracks will still be there.
I may not find all the tiny pieces.
Only you GOD can put things back together perfectly.
I want to handle my mate carefully.
I realize the value of our relationship.
I want to be faithful in this, Father.
I know that if I drop it you will catch it.
Your hands will protect it from destruction.
I want to always handle my porcelain treasure carefully,
gently, and lovingly.
Then as years wear on its value is without measure.
GOD what a priceless treasure my mate is.

Graduating To Go Further

You've graduated me from school LORD.
The school that prepares us for our ministries.
I look around and so many are still there.
Some will be career students and others are not ready
to graduate.
In a vision you have shown me that
I have left some in school.
I'm happy to go higher in you GOD.
Now I just want to have my assignment.
Now I just want to get my first job.
Now I want to go to work for you.

The Sting of Death

LORD, the loss of a loved one carries such grief.
Death can cause so much pain.
We hate to release those we love.
Releasing is the only way to go forward.
The loss we feel leaves us so empty.
We have to mourn our loss.
We hope that our loved ones are in a better place.
We know that they will not suffer on this earth anymore.
We truly hope that they are in a better place,
A place where we someday hope to be.
In the mean time our lives have an emptiness that no one
can fill.
It is there until our death.
When it is time for us to die we will leave emptiness in the
lives of those we leave behind.
The pain that we feel only time can heal.
We must remember to let go.
Holding on puts a part of our lives on hold.
We must let go and move ahead.

The Movie

I sit and look at this movie.
I see the actors and actresses.
There is something familiar about the star.
There is something about the walk.
The movement.
I look into the heart and it seems so strange.
I look into the mind and still I can't recall.
I look deep inside the soul.
Something is hidden there.
I look deeper still.
I see that it's me.
This is me!
The story is a flash of the past.
I see it scene by scene.
I became a total stranger to myself.
I became someone who had lost all identity.
Who was I LORD?
I look back over my life as if looking at a move.
It's quite a sad movie.
I am ashamed of who I was.
So much hurt.
So much pain.
So much frustration.

Fighting Saints

I fight and I war LORD.
I battle great strongholds.
I pray fervently for souls.
I bless your people and I curse demons.
Father this is a mighty war to fight.
What is the most difficult battle of this war?
What makes my spirit grieve?
It's not the men or women of the world.
It's the men or women of Christ.
They give place to spirits that they should not entertain.
Still they provide lodging for satan and his eunuchs.
LORD my greatest war is with saints under strongholds.

The Breath of Life

My desire LORD is to have obedience and submission be
natural to me.
I desire them to be as natural as inhaling and exhaling.
Just as I inhale and exhale to breathe,
I desire to have obedience as I inhale and submission as I
exhale.
My breath is the life of me.
If I do not breathe I die.
Obedience and Submission are the life of my spirituality.
Without them I am nothing.
As I inhale it becomes submission
As I exhale it becomes obedience.
I live and my spirituality lives.

My Heart's Desire

I long to share my dreams GOD.
I want to release my joy.
Things happen in my life,
There is no one to share it with.
I want to celebrate the good time with someone.
I want to cry in someone's arms.
Father, I long for a companion.
I want someone special in my life.
I want to be able to share all my successes.
I want to share all of my failures.
It is so difficult to hold it all inside.
It screams inside me.
I want to hear the voice of a special friend say
"congratulations".
I long to feel the embrace.
GOD, I desire to have my special companion.
I have so much to say and no one to say it to.
Who is the one that will rejoice when I rejoice?
Who will caress me when I cry?
There is such emptiness in my life.
Please GOD fill that void.
Fill it with that very special companion that I desire.

The Rainbow

A rainbow of promises GOD.
There are so many blessings stored.
When the floodgates open
It will be so overwhelming.
I've seen things great and small.
Promises shown to me by you.
I want to walk down the path to receive these blessings.
What a beautiful sight a rainbow is.
All of your promises are true.
You are a GOD who keeps promises.

Obedience Not Vanity

At times it seems as if the more I obey you the more
trouble I get into.
It starts to seem as if I'm doing everything wrong.
The despair is like a ton of steel.
I cry out to you to show me.
I cry out to you to help me.
I cry out to you to guide me.
Still I seem to be sitting alone under the gourd plant.
I only want to obey.
I want to know that I've done what you told me to do.
I want to glorify you GOD.
If I do this all the pain and despair is not vanity.
It is for you GOD.

I RECEIVE

Dear GOD:
With all my heart I do receive
Everything in your word because I do believe.
I receive the anointing you've placed in my life.
I open myself up without misery and strife.
I receive the love Jesus had for me
Because on the cross he died you see.
I receive your gentle caring arms of protection
Because deep within me you're working perfection.
I receive this feeling deep in my soul
That makes me aim and achieve spiritual goals.
All your spiritual blessings I do receive
Because for them my heart did grieve.
I receive the renewing you've placed in my mind,
Because I have no desire to follow the blind.
I receive the love you've placed in my heart
Dear GOD it's a love that will never depart.
I receive the time you've spent with me
Because dear GOD it's not vain--
you'll see.
In Jesus name I receive all of this
And now my LORD I'll close with a kiss
Now receive this kiss as it comes your way
Just as I have received so much from you today.

                                    WITH ALL MY LOVE

One Body

We spend so much time in denominational wars.
We want to convert others to our denomination.
Why can't we accept everyone in Christ as part of the body of Christ?
Instead the hand tells the foot how to walk,
The eyes tell the ears how to hear,
The feet tell the nose how to smell.
If everyone would do their best to perfect their purpose, the body would benefit tremendously.
If we would love each other as a sister or brother, perhaps our body (Christ's) would not be so filled with corruption.
Each member together forms the perfect body of Christ.
Love is the skin that covers the body.
We are all under the covering of love.

Please Pluck The Weeds

Father I feel as though I was a beautiful flower.
Standing alone.
Weeds grew all around me.
They took all the sunshine from me.
They towered over me.
No one could see me for the weeds.
What a sad state I was in.
Finally GOD you plucked out the weeds.
Some you pulled out from the root.
Others the root wasn't taken out the first time.
When you pluck them out this time they will never grow again.
Now the flower is starting to look beautiful again.
Now there is much to see.
GOD, thank you for your love.
Thank you for seeing the beauty in me.

A Seer

The gift of a seer is powerful.
You can see birth.
You can see death.
You can see pain.
You can see joy.
As a seer you see into the heart of man.
You can see the evil that they try to hide.
You can see the good and modesty often concealed.
The gift of a seer carries much responsibility.
You must know when to speak.
You must know when to keep quiet.
As a seer you can bless and you can curse.
Blessing is fun and exciting.
As a seer I desire to bless.
Being a seer is to love GOD and HIS people.

Excitement and Glory

GOD, you are the most awesome of awesome.
My exuberance overwhelms me.
I just love you GOD.
You are absolutely magnificent.
No love can touch my love for you.
All love illuminates from my love for you.
Oh, My GOD, My GOD.
I just praise your name.
Glory, Hallelujah!!
What a mighty GOD you are
Words can never do you justice
Father; I'm inept to speak.
I Do Love You.

I Stand Firm

I stand firm on your Word, GOD.
I trust you with all my heart.
I make mistakes every day,
but I continue in my walk.
Christianity is a beautiful life.
Sometimes I give a word of encouragement,
sometimes it's just a smile,
but I share it somehow.
I may simply say I love GOD,
Even when times are hard.
You are always on my mind.
Father, I am planted firm.
My growth is in good ground.
I desire to bring forth fruit.
Neither the fowls of the air,
Nor the harshness of weather can hinder my growth.
My growth represents my love
My love is true.
LORD I Stand Firm.

The Hurt

Oh LORD, I feel so much pain.
It's rooted deep in my heart.
I've gone over this time and again.
It pierces me like a dart.

Tell me LORD, what must I do,
To take away my sorrow?
Dear GOD, I cry out to you.
Please give me hope for tomorrow.

I want to hear every word you say,
because that will ease my pain.
Your tender voice I want to obey,
In this I have much to gain.

Dear GOD, take away all my hurt.
Root it up and cast it out.
I ask you for all this is worth.
Let me feel the release without doubt.

Father, I know that you are faithful and just.
I know that you are taking the pain.
In you, Dear GOD, I'll always trust.
You will answer me once again.

Mustard Seed Faith

GOD has given to each of us a measure of faith.
This is our gift from heaven above.
When we're tried if we would just wait.
Then we would see the wonder of GOD's true love.

We experience many different things in life.
Some leave us with hurt, pain, bitterness or remorse.
If only we would place our faith in GOD without strife.
Then without a doubt we'll know that we made the right choice.

We should labor to increase our faith every day.
And believe in GOD more and more.
Then when fiery trials come our way.
That faith will stand before us at the door.

A mustard seed is so very small,
And so is our child like faith.
But that mustard seed grows to be very tall.
So belief in GOD is all it takes.

If only we could have mustard seed faith.
We would start out with so little and then, see it grow.
That little bit of faith is all it takes.
But first believe in Jesus and that through GOD he arose.

Don't Give Up

I just want to try to do my best.
Every day I'll try a little harder.
Every day I'll go a little further.
I just want to be the best that I can be.
The hills get steep sometimes,
But I see your angel with his outstretched hand.
The water gets muddy at times,
But I see the safety of the shore.
The darkness can sometimes frighten me,
But I know that daylight will come.
The test of my faith is to not give up.
This walk is not just daily, but minute by minute.
My hope lies in GOD.
This hope keeps my faith alive.
When trouble seems to come on every side,
I stand firm in my hope.
The hills become level plains.
The muddy water becomes as clear as glass.
The darkness turns into a day of sunshine.
I will not give up.

Your Friend Forever

Jesus,

I want to thank you.
I thank you for being my confident,
I thank you for being my friend,
I thank you for being by brother,
I thank you for being my intercessor,
I thank you for being my savior.
I want to thank you Jesus for taking all the bad and awful things of my life and holding them in the palm of your hands.
I want to thank you for taking those things and casting them into the sea.
I want to thank you Jesus for everything.

Sincerely,

Your Friend Forever,

Dear GOD I Love You

I really don't think that the heavens or the earth can
contain my love for you.
My heart yearns to express this love.
All I can do is love your people and serve them.
This is the only way I can begin to show my love.
Even this can't express what I feel.
Doing more means seeking a holy life.
Yet this also seems ineffective.
Still I will labor daily to show my love.
Dear GOD I Love You.

No Homestead Here

The old man lurks.
He creeps about.
He peers around corners.
He seeks any opportunity to come in.
He brings death and destruction.
He also has illness and disease.
The old man is so very old.
He wants to live again.
The only way he can live is to come into your home.
He wants to declare homestead right.
Once in, he will go into every room and claim it.
He will become so very comfortable.
If successful, he will be more difficult to expel than before.
The old man is the former you.
Our home is our spiritual lives, our bodies, souls, and minds.
It is the flesh that you crucified on the cross.
He has no claim on your home.
The homestead law is ineffective in our spiritual world.
We must know the law!
We must know our rights!
We must take authority over our home!
We must demand that the intruder leave!
Further still, we must demand that he never ever return!
The old man no longer has an invitation into our home.
We must be in control!
We must take authority!
WE MUST STAND!

Selah

SEEK THE SPIRITUAL
AND
GOD WILL REWARD THE MATERIAL

because

GOD *IS* **LORD** OF
JESUS AND ALL!